curious about

RABBITS

T0004827

BY JILL SHERMAN

AMICUS • AMICUS INK

What are you

curious about?

CHAPTER THREE

Rabbit Behavior
PAGE
14

Curious About is published
by Amicus and Amicus Ink
P.O. Box 227
Mankato, MN 56002
www.amicuspublishing.us

Editor: Alissa Thielges
Series Designer: Kathleen Petelinsek
Book Designer: Ciara Beitlich
Photo researcher: Bridget Prehn

Library of Congress Cataloging-in-Publication Data
Names: Sherman, Jill, author.
Title: Curious about rabbits / by Jill Sherman.
Description: Mankato : Amicus, [2021] | Series: Curious
about pets | Includes bibliographical references and index.
| Audience: Ages 6–9 | Audience: Grades 2–3
Identifiers: LCCN 2019053812 (print) | LCCN 2019053813
(ebook) | ISBN 9781681519708 (library binding) | ISBN
9781681526171 (paperback) | ISBN 9781645490555 (pdf)
Subjects: LCSH: Rabbits—Juvenile literature.
Classification: LCC SF453.2 .S535 2021 (print) | LCC
SF453.2 (ebook) | DDC 636.932/2—dc23
LC record available at https://lccn.loc.gov/2019053812
LC ebook record available at https://lccn.loc.gov/2019053813

Photos © Dreamstime/Isselee cover, 1; Shutterstock/
StoneMonkeyswk 2 (left), 5; Shutterstock/Peyker 2 (right), 11;
Flickr/4thirdsOpticalDelusions 3, 15; iStock/Neniya 6; Alamy/
Adam Ján Figel 7; Alamy/Joe Blossom 8–9; Shutterstock/Sven
Boettcher 10; Shutterstock/Linas T 12–13; iStock/GlobalP 16;
Shutterstock/Photobac 17, KanphotoSS 19 (top), Boonchuay1970
19 (lettuce), Volosina 19 (berries), Pakhnyushchy 19 (cucumber),
kikpokemon 20, Dorottya Mathe 21 (Lionhead), Robynrg 21 (mini
lop), Eric Isselee 21 (Rex), Jostein Hauge 21 (Netherland dwarf),
pets in frames 21 (Polish)

Printed in the United States of America

Do pet rabbits make a lot of sounds?

Rabbits are usually quiet. But they do make soft sounds. A happy pet rabbit might purr, hum, or even cluck! It sounds like a chicken, but much quieter. An unhappy rabbit might growl, hiss, or whimper.

Rabbits communicate with sounds and body language.

Leafy greens are a healthy rabbit treat.

My rabbit made a honking noise. What does that mean?

DID YOU KNOW?

Rabbits can birth a new litter every month. A litter can have 4 to 12 baby bunnies.

Your bunny is excited. Is she eating a special treat? Yum! Honking can also mean, "I'm looking for love!" Your bunny may want a **mate**. If you don't want baby bunnies, make sure you have two females or two males.

CHAPTER TWO

Why does my rabbit thump its back leg?

Thump-thump-thump! Your rabbit is scared or nervous. Thumping is LOUD. In the wild, this tells other rabbits that danger is nearby. A scared rabbit may also flatten its ears and shiver. It will run away and hide if it can.

DID YOU KNOW?
Rabbits can hear sounds almost 2 miles (3.2 km) away.

Why is my rabbit jumping in the air?

This is the happiest rabbit behavior. It is called a **binky**. A rabbit will jump in the air and twist its body. It looks pretty strange. But it's a rabbit's way of saying it loves its life with you.

A happy rabbit does a binky, just like a happy person may do a dance.

Why does my rabbit kick?

Rabbits kick when they are annoyed. If a rabbit kicks, it is trying to get away. If you are holding a kicking rabbit, put it down gently. A rabbit's spine is fragile. A rabbit can hurt its back if it kicks too hard while being held.

A rabbit that kicks while hopping away is upset.

Why does my rabbit rub its chin on things?

It is marking its **territory**. A rabbit has scent **glands** under its chin. By rubbing, it leaves its scent. It is saying, "This is mine!" This is called chinning. If your rabbit rubs its chin on you, it likes you a lot.

Rabbits rub their chins on
things to leave their scent.

Do rabbits only hop around?

No. Rabbits sometimes walk. They do this when exploring a new place. But rabbits prefer hopping. It's easier. Their strong back legs were made for it. Hopping is the fastest way to get around. A bunny can move as fast as 50 miles (80 km) per hour!

| 0ft | 1ft 0.3m | 2ft 0.6m | 3ft 0.9m | 4ft 1.2m |

5ft	6ft	7ft	8ft	9ft	10ft
1.5m	1.8m	2.1m	2.4m	2.7m	3.0m

Why are rabbits always chewing on things?

Rabbits need to chew. Their teeth are always growing. Chewing keeps the teeth short and healthy. What's safe to chew on? Fresh hay is best. It makes up 90 percent of a rabbit's **diet**. Rabbit toys or cardboard also work.

Make sure your rabbit has plenty of hay to chew on.

SAFE TREATS FOR RABBITS

Lettuce

Berries

Cucumbers

Could a pet rabbit survive in the wild?

A healthy rabbit can live 8 to 12 years.

No. Pet rabbits wouldn't last long on their own. They've never had to find food or shelter. They haven't had to escape from **predators**. Pet rabbits are safest and happiest when they are well cared for. An indoor cage with a hiding place is a good home.

LIONHEAD

MINI LOP

REX

NETHERLAND DWARF

POLISH

ASK MORE QUESTIONS

I want a rabbit. What kind would be best for me?

🐾

What kinds of things do I need to care for a rabbit?

🐾

Try a BIG QUESTION: How do I bond with my rabbit?

SEARCH FOR ANSWERS

Search the library catalog or the Internet.
A librarian, teacher, or parent can help you.

Using Keywords
Find the looking glass.

🔍

Keywords are the most important words in your question.

❓

If you want to know about:
- different kinds of rabbits, type: RABBIT BREEDS
- how to take care of a rabbit, type: RABBIT CARE

FIND GOOD SOURCES

Here are some good, safe sources you can use in your research.
Your librarian can help you find more.

Books

Bunnies from Head to Tail
by Emmett Martin, 2021.

Is a Rabbit a Good Pet for Me?
by Melissa Rae Shofner, 2020.

Internet Sites

American Rabbit Breeders Association (ARBA)
https://arba.net/recognized-breeds/
The ARBA is a national organization of people who raise rabbits. It is a good source for rabbit information.

House Rabbit Society
https://rabbit.org/living-with-a-house-rabbit-2/
The House Rabbit Society helps find homes for pet rabbits. It has information on rabbit care.

Every effort has been made to ensure that these websites are appropriate for children. However, because of the nature of the Internet, it is impossible to guarantee that these sites will remain active indefinitely or that their contents will not be altered.

SHARE AND TAKE ACTION

Visit a friend or local breeder that cares for rabbits.
How are they cared for?

With an adult, volunteer at a rabbit rescue.
You could also help raise money for one.

Teach others about rabbit care.

Be safe around rabbits.
Learn their body language so that you can treat them with care.

GLOSSARY

binky When a rabbit jumps into the air and twists its body.

diet What an animal eats.

gland An organ in the body that makes chemicals or releases a fluid or smell.

mate One of a breeding pair of animals.

predator An animal that hunts other animals for food.

territory An area that an animal uses for hunting or finding food.

INDEX

About the Author

Jill Sherman is a children's book author living in Brooklyn, New York. She has a pet dog named Reed, whom she spoils endlessly. Reed prefers cuddling on the couch to playing at the dog park, and Jill is perfectly happy with that.